CONTENTS

ZOOM INTO...

...the emerald-green world of plants and imagine that you could shrink to the size of an ant and wander through jungles of grass, climb mountains of moss and sip the sweet nectar from a flowery cup. Get ready to discover some fascinating facts and become closer than close to plants with amazing ZOOMs!

Zoom in

If you looked at a drop of pond water through a microscope, you might see some mini-monsters wriggling about. Thanks to the power of the magnifying lens, you are looking at simple plants called **algae**. A microscope uses lenses to magnify the image of very small things, often several hundred times. Modern microscopes may use other techniques to magnify objects many thousands of times.

So close

Plants with the ACTUAL SIZE icons are shown at their real-life size, as though they're actually on the page! Comparing the plant with a standard paperclip really helps you to understand its size.

ACTUAL SIZE

ZOOM x4

Macro photography

The art of taking pictures of small things in close-up is called macro photography. Using these, and other techniques, photographers and scientists have helped us to get a better understanding of the ways that plants and animals live.

Try it

WHAT IS IT? images let you use your new investigation skills to guess what the plant might be. Then just turn over the page to find out that IT IS…

ZOOM x1750

WHAt iS it?

ENERGY MACHINES

We need plants because they take the energy in sunlight and convert it into food. It is a process called **photosynthesis**. While they are performing this fabulous feat, plants make **oxygen**, which is the gas we use to turn food back into energy. So, without plants, we could neither eat nor breathe!

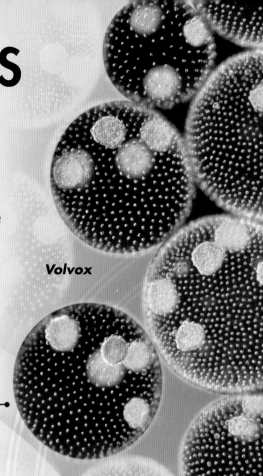

Volvox

Each Volvox is just one cell.

The colony is held inside a jelly-like wall.

ZOOM x100

The smallest plants

*Living things are made up of building blocks called **cells**. Huge trees are made of billions of cells, but the simplest plants, such as Volvox, are just one cell. These plants are called algae (say: al-ghee), and they live in water. Millions of strands of the algae Spirogyra (left) create slimy, green pond scum.*

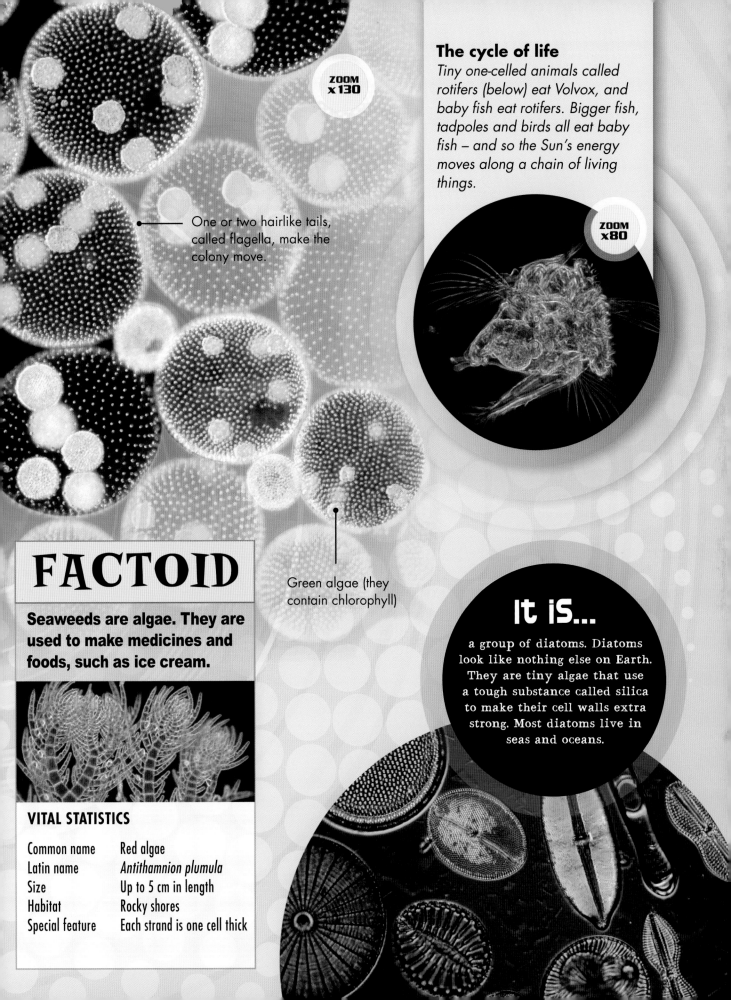

ZOOM x130

One or two hairlike tails, called flagella, make the colony move.

The cycle of life

Tiny one-celled animals called rotifers (below) eat Volvox, and baby fish eat rotifers. Bigger fish, tadpoles and birds all eat baby fish – and so the Sun's energy moves along a chain of living things.

ZOOM x80

Green algae (they contain chlorophyll)

FACTOID

Seaweeds are algae. They are used to make medicines and foods, such as ice cream.

It is...

a group of diatoms. Diatoms look like nothing else on Earth. They are tiny algae that use a tough substance called silica to make their cell walls extra strong. Most diatoms live in seas and oceans.

VITAL STATISTICS

Common name	Red algae
Latin name	*Antithamnion plumula*
Size	Up to 5 cm in length
Habitat	Rocky shores
Special feature	Each strand is one cell thick

TOWERS AND TUBES

Plants have important jobs to do. They position themselves to grab as much sunshine as possible, so they can photosynthesize and grow. They collect water from the soil, make food and move **nutrients** around. When you zoom inside a plant you can see exactly how it is able to carry out these essential tasks.

ACTUAL SIZE

Super highways

Stems work like strong but bendy towers, raising the leaves away from the soil so they can reach more light. They connect the food production areas – the leaves – with the plant's roots, flowers and fruits. Nutrients, such as minerals, food and water, travel along them.

ZOOM x800

WHAT IS it?

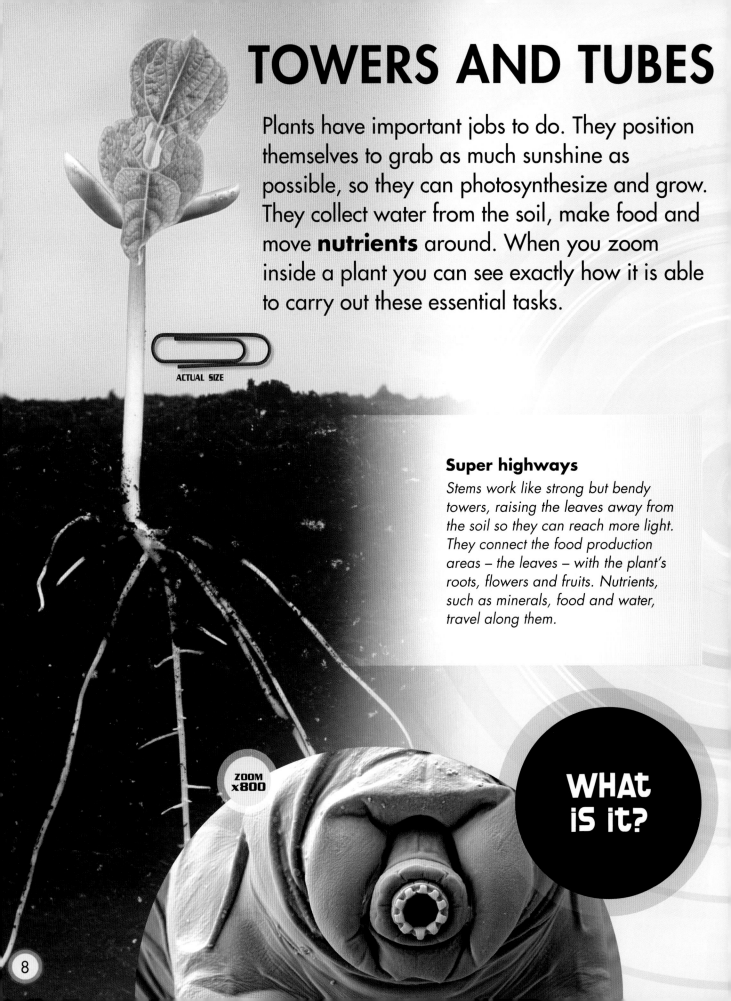

Inside stems

Long tubes run the length of the stems. Some tubes carry water from the roots to the plant. They are called xylem vessels. Others carry food, mostly in the form of sugar, around the plant. They are called phloem tubes (say: flo-em).

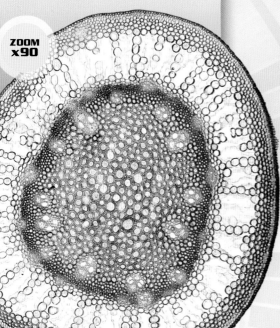

ZOOM x90

Bendy bamboo

Air spaces between the cells keep the stem strong, but light and flexible. Bamboo stems have large hollow centres, and some types can grow up to 30 metres in height.

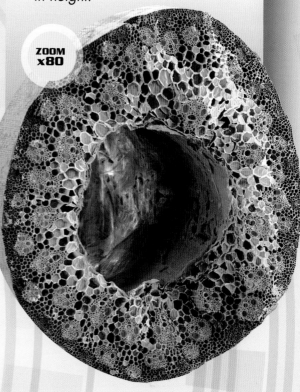

ZOOM x80

ZOOM x260

Staying strong

Simple plant cells are packed together like boxes. Each cell has **cellulose** in its walls, to make the plant strong. The dark area in a cell is the nucleus – it is the plant's control centre.

MOSS MOUNTAINS

Some of our planet's most amazing plants are ones we walk on, or over, without even noticing them. Mosses, for example, look just like bouncy, green cushions – until you zoom in on them. They can grow several metres wide, or may be so small that they can be seen only with a microscope.

Spore capsules fire spores into the air.

The leaves collect water.

FACTOID

Mosses have been around for about 300 million years, and there are more than 12,000 species, or types.

VITAL STATISTICS

Common name	Marsh moss
Latin name	*Sphagnum*
Size	10–40 mm in height
Habitat	Wet places
Special feature	Can hold lots of water in its structure

It is...

a water bear or moss piglet, and it hides in moss. It looks fearsome, but it's tiny: this image is magnified 220 times. If it dries out, a water bear can survive for ten years, 'frozen' in time until it gets wet again.

Lighter than air

Tiny moss **spores** have a tough outer coat to protect them. They are so small and light that they can float away on the lightest breeze.

ZOOM
x1000

ZOOM
x2

Moss

Exploding plants

The first plants that grew on land had no flowers or **seeds**. Today's mosses, **liverworts** and **ferns** are related to those early plants, and they also produce spores instead of seeds. Zoom into this moss and you can see tall stalks, called sporophytes. Each capsule at the top of a sporophyte holds thousands of spores.

ZOOM
x10

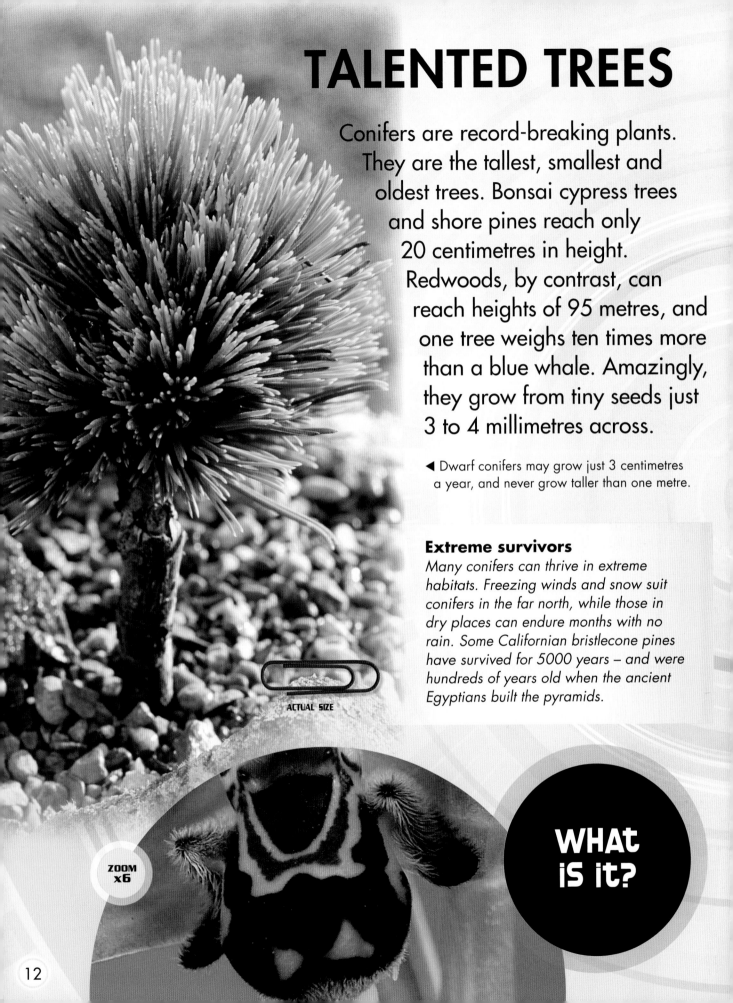

TALENTED TREES

Conifers are record-breaking plants. They are the tallest, smallest and oldest trees. Bonsai cypress trees and shore pines reach only 20 centimetres in height. Redwoods, by contrast, can reach heights of 95 metres, and one tree weighs ten times more than a blue whale. Amazingly, they grow from tiny seeds just 3 to 4 millimetres across.

◄ Dwarf conifers may grow just 3 centimetres a year, and never grow taller than one metre.

ACTUAL SIZE

Extreme survivors

Many conifers can thrive in extreme habitats. Freezing winds and snow suit conifers in the far north, while those in dry places can endure months with no rain. Some Californian bristlecone pines have survived for 5000 years – and were hundreds of years old when the ancient Egyptians built the pyramids.

ZOOM x6

WHAT IS it?

Saving water

Conifer leaves are usually shaped like needles or scales, and coated with a waxy layer. This helps them to save water and survive in cold weather. Most conifers are evergreen, which means they don't lose their leaves every year.

ACTUAL SIZE

Magic numbers

Pinecone scales are arranged in two sets of spirals – one anti-clockwise, and one clockwise. The number of spirals follows a unique mathematical sequence of numbers, called the **Fibonacci series**. It is the best way to pack in lots of scales, evenly and without gaps.

ZOOM x3

Cones and seeds

One conifer tree grows both male and female cones. The yellow **pollen** on these little male cones will be carried, by wind, to the bigger female cones. The pollen **fertilizes** their eggs, but it takes up to three years for a female cone to mature. Once the seeds are grown, they fall to the ground.

ZOOM x2

FLOWERS IN FANCY DRESS

Trek through a rainforest and you will be surrounded by green. Huge emerald leaves, dangling green **creepers** and frilly fern **fronds** fill every space. Then your eye will catch the dazzling display of flowers, nestled in the crook of a tree. Showy, colourful and scented – flowers put on a bold display for a reason.

Orchid

ZOOM x2

Big flower or little flowers?

*How big is a sunflower flower? You might think it is as big as your hand, or even bigger. Zoom in, and you will see that one sunflower head actually contains hundreds of flowers, each called a **floret** and no larger than your fingernail. One floret can produce one seed.*

ACTUAL SIZE

One petal, shaped like a landing platform, leads the insect toward the **nectary**.

It is...

a bee orchid. These flowers look and smell like female bees. When male bees try to mate with the flower, pollen rubs off on their back, which they accidentally transfer to other flowers.

Sugary liquid is produced in the nectary to attract insects.

Bright, colourful petals attract insects.

Pollen is carried on stamens. It brushes onto an insect that passes by.

The stigma is connected to the **ovary**, which contains a flower's eggs.

FACTOID

The world's largest flowers are Rafflesias, and they stink of rotting meat. One flower can measure 90 centimetres wide.

VITAL STATISTICS

Common name	Orchid
Latin name	*Family Orchidaceae*
Size	Up to 250 cm in height
Habitat	Mostly in warm, damp places
Special feature	Beautiful flowers

ZOOM x3

Secrets inside

*Scientists zoom into a plant's insides to understand how it reproduces. This flower has been cut in half, lengthways, to reveal its hidden reproductive organs. Long pollen-tipped **stamens** surround the carpel, which protects the tiny, round eggs that are nestling inside its fleshy tissues.*

PLANTS ON THE MOVE

When animals want to mate, it's easy. They can walk, swim or fly to find the perfect partner. Plants, however, are usually rooted to the ground. They overcome this problem by sending tiny parts of themselves – pollen – out into the world.

ZOOM x5

◀ Tiny granules of orange pollen coat the **anthers** of a lily flower. The anthers are the top part of a stamen.

What is pollen?

Pollen contains male sex cells, which combine with female sex cells, or eggs, to make seeds. When pollen lands on a **stigma** – the female part of a flower – **pollination** has taken place. The pollen grows a tube down the stigma to reach the ovary, and then combines with an egg inside. This is called fertilization.

Tough travellers

Some pollen grains are ribbed, or spiked; others are round, oval, flat or plump. It all depends on which plant they come from. The outer rind of a pollen grain is so tough it can survive for tens of thousands of years. One flower may produce thousands of pollen grains.

ZOOM x1000

Perfect pollinators

Pollen grains are small, which means they can travel easily – often on the wind. Many flowering plants rely on insects, such as this chafer beetle, for pollination. As they feed on plants the bugs get covered in pollen, which then rubs off onto stigmas.

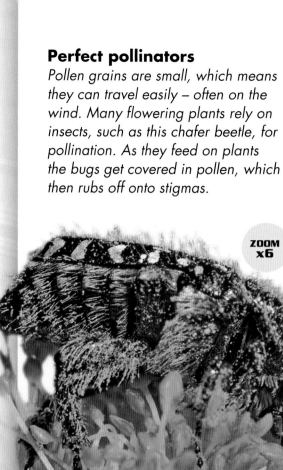

ZOOM x6

Super small

Zoom into this flower anther to see little green grains of pollen. The smallest pollen grains are just 20 nanometres wide. One nanometre is a millionth of a millimetre!

ZOOM x70

ZOOM x5

WHAt iS it?

SEED JOURNEYS

Plants do not make caring parents. Once they have produced their seeds, most plants want their offspring to go as far away as possible! They don't want to be fighting for space, light and water. So they produce seeds that are well equipped to go on a long journey – by one means or another!

The pappus lifts the seed up in wind.

Each seed is attached so lightly to the plant that the smallest breeze will lift it up.

FACTOID

According to folklore, the number of puffs it takes to blow all the seeds off a dandelion seedhead tells you the time of day. Four puffs means it is four o'clock in the afternoon.

VITAL STATISTICS

Common name	Dandelion
Latin name	*Taraxacum officinale*
Size	5 to 20 cm in height
Habitat	Grassland and wasteland
Special feature	Each flowerhead can have more than 150 florets

ZOOM x2.5

Juicy fruits
After fertilization, some ovaries grow into fruits, or berries. Animals eat the fruits, and the seeds inside pass through their body, coming out in their faeces (say: fee-sees). In the right conditions, the seeds will germinate and grow into new plants.

Dandelion

ZOOM x3

New beginnings
When a seed has the right conditions of water, soil and temperature, it may begin to grow a root, and eventually develop into a new plant. This is called **germination**.

ZOOM x6

The fine hairs are called the pappus.

It is...
a burdock flower. Seeds develop inside the tough capsules, or burrs. Little hooks on a burr attach it to a passing animal, or person, and it is carried to a new place where the seeds may have the right conditions to grow.

GREEN DEFENDERS

Many animals, including us, know that plants can make tasty, healthy food. To survive, plants have some clever ways to defend themselves. Red yew berries look tasty, but are poisonous to some animals, and hard nuts are impossible for all but the strongest beaks to break.

Prickly plant

The peculiar shape of a cactus helps this prickly plant cope in a challenging environment. Sharp spines cover large green pads that look like giant leaves. In fact, the spines are leaves, and the pads are swollen stems. The stems store water – essential in a dry habitat where it rarely rains.

Sharp and cutting

Spines, spikes, prickles and thorns are a first line of defence for many plants. It would take a brave animal to place its jaws around a hairy mary plant. Each stem is smothered in needle-pointed spines, measuring up to 8 centimetres in length.

ACTUAL SIZE

Transferring poison

Milkweed produces toxic (poisonous) juice, or sap, which is deadly to most insects. Monarch caterpillars, however, eat the plant and store the deadly chemicals in their own body, making them poisonous to the animals that feed on them.

ZOOM x3

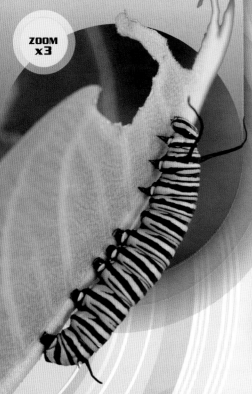

Toxic ooze

Storing poisonous chemicals in their tissues is another crafty way to deter hungry creatures. Rubber trees make sticky latex. It is toxic, but also traps insects trying to feed on the tree.

Plant attack

Hairs on a nettle leaf are tipped with tiny beads of **silica** (left). If you brush against the leaf, the tips will snap off and the hairs will spear your skin, injecting foul chemicals. One chemical causes pain, while another makes the skin swollen, red and itchy. Even grasses contain sharp pieces of silica.

ZOOM x100

WHAT IS IT?

ZOOM x4

MEAT-EATING PLANTS

When you look closely at plants, you begin to discover that they hold some strange, but deadly secrets. In the endless battle for survival, animals usually turn plants into food – but in some rare cases, plants are the winners because they actually eat animals!

Red colour and sweet-smelling nectar attract insects.

ZOOM x2

FACTOID

Small flies can escape from the traps. This means the plant only spends time and energy on digesting larger meaty meals.

VITAL STATISTICS

Common name	Venus flytrap
Latin name	*Dionaea muscipula*
Size	Leaves are 5 to 30 cm in length
Habitat	Damp, mossy places
Special feature	The traps are closed for up to ten days, while a bug is digested

Extreme measures
The leaves of pitcher plants form colourful cups to attract insects. Curious bugs fall into the cups, which contain a potion of water and flesh-dissolving chemicals.

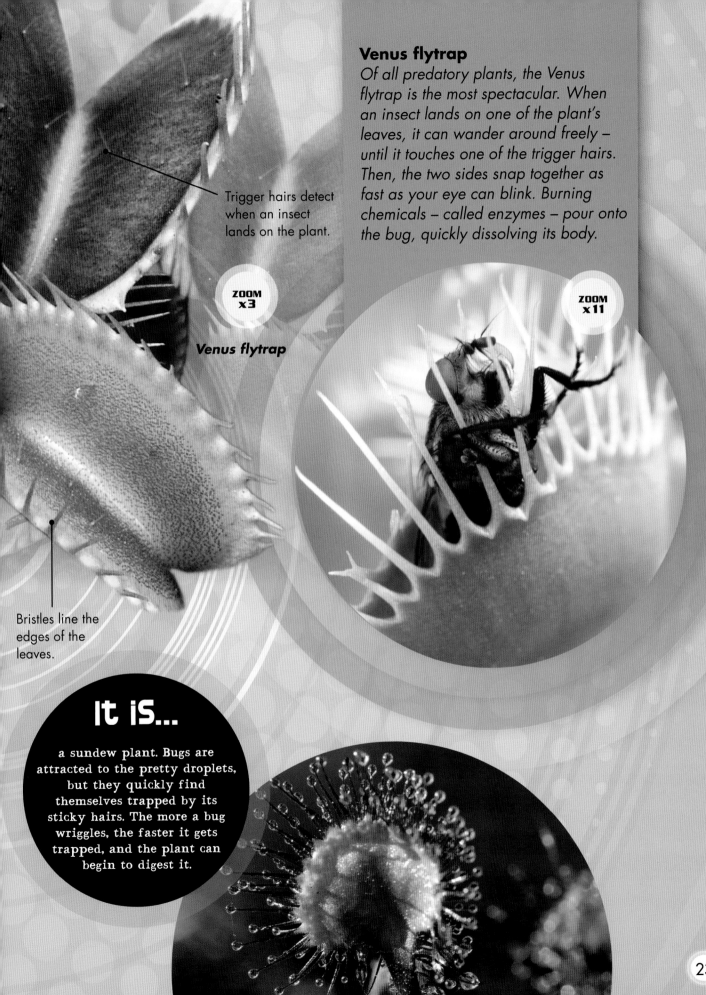

Trigger hairs detect when an insect lands on the plant.

ZOOM x3

Venus flytrap

Venus flytrap

Of all predatory plants, the Venus flytrap is the most spectacular. When an insect lands on one of the plant's leaves, it can wander around freely – until it touches one of the trigger hairs. Then, the two sides snap together as fast as your eye can blink. Burning chemicals – called enzymes – pour onto the bug, quickly dissolving its body.

ZOOM x11

Bristles line the edges of the leaves.

It is...

a sundew plant. Bugs are attracted to the pretty droplets, but they quickly find themselves trapped by its sticky hairs. The more a bug wriggles, the faster it gets trapped, and the plant can begin to digest it.

PLANT PARTNERS

Animals and plants depend on each other. Most animals eat plants, but many plants get something out of the relationship, too. Peer closely into the complex world of nature, and you will find out how living things often live in a strange kind of harmony.

Favouring fruit

Fruit bats do trees two big favours. When they feed on pollen, bats accidentally pollinate the flowers – which causes fruits to grow. They also disperse the tree's seeds by eating the fruits. The seeds pass through their body, and emerge in faeces, ready to grow into new plants.

WHAT IS IT?

ZOOM x8

Agouti

These rodents are the only animals that are able to open the tough outer husk of a brazil nut. Agoutis have extremely strong incisor teeth, which keep growing throughout their lives. Brazil nut trees rely on agoutis to spread their seeds and if these rodents, which are endangered, died out, so would the trees.

Civet coffee

Palm civets enjoy the taste of juicy berries that grow on coffee plants. The seeds are partly digested, passed out as faeces and may germinate. In a strange twist, the seeds – coffee beans – are collected by people to be ground up and used to brew a delicious type of coffee – the most expensive in the world.

ZOOM
x 10

Taking in lodgers

Acacia trees love having ants to stay. Ants not only attack insect pests, they even destroy nearby plants that might take light or water from the acacia. In return, the tree rewards its ants by making little orange beads of food on their leaves. Ants feed the beads to their larvae (young).

FRUITING FUNGI

When is a plant not a plant? When it is a fungus. These strange living things lead a very different life to green plants. Instead of using light to make food, fungi feed on living things or the remains of dead things. Mushrooms, **mould** and yeast are different types of fungus.

Fly agaric

ZOOM x2

Going underground

Fungi don't have roots. They have tiny feeding threads, called hyphae (say: hi-fee), which grow through soil, or the animal or plant they are feeding on. The hyphae absorb nutrients and can spread into dense networks that cover huge distances underground, making them the biggest living things on Earth.

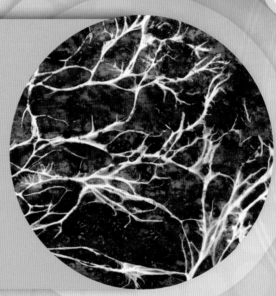

It is...

a lichen. Scientists once thought lichens were types of plant, until they zoomed in close and discovered that a lichen is actually made up of a fungus and an alga living together.

The cap protects the gills, where spores are produced.

Fly agaric is the white-spotted red toadstool that is often illustrated in fairytales and other picture books.

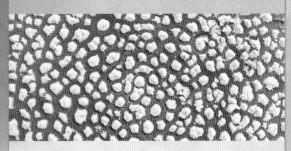

VITAL STATISTICS

Common name	Fly agaric
Latin name	*Amanita muscaria*
Size	8–10 cm in length
Habitat	Under birch and spruce trees
Special feature	Poisonous and should NEVER be tasted

The fruiting body usually grows upwards, so the spores can disperse.

Heads in the air

The part of a fungus we can usually spot, such as a mushroom, is called the fruiting body. It makes millions of microscopic spores that drift in the air. Bracket fungi grow huge fruiting spores on trees and rotting wood. The tiniest fruiting bodies are often moulds, and are microscopic in size.

ZOOM x3000

USE YOUR EYES

Use your eyes to study these zooms that appear throughout the book. Can you recognize any of them just by looking at them? Are there any clues, such as colour or shape, that help you work out where you've seen these images before?

1 *I am a super-strong alga with silica to toughen me up.*

2 *Isn't nature brilliant? Look how neatly I am packed together, but what am I?*

3 *We may be tiny, but we are tough and can survive long journeys. We often travel by insect!*

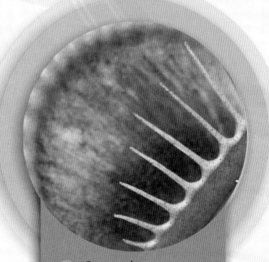

4 *Ouch, these prickly spines have an important job to do.*

5 *Come close, we are snappy to see you!*

6 Small and tasty, we appeal to ants. What are we?

7 Huge needle-like spines cover my stems. I look scary!

8 I may be pretty but I hide a deep, dark secret. Do you know what I am?

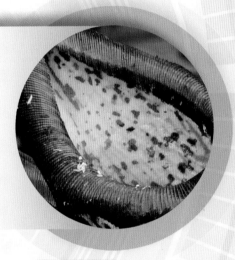

9 Cut me in half, take a super-thin slice and put me under a microscope.

10 Gently blow and use me to tell the time.

11 My good looks appeal to people, but I want to impress those beautiful bees.

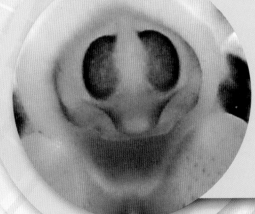

Answers: 1. p7 2. p13 3. p17 4. p20 5. p22 6. p25 7. p20 8. p22 9. p9 10. p18 11. p14

29

GLOSSARY

Algae Simple plants that photosynthesize, but do not have true stems and roots. Algae do not grow flowers. Seaweeds are algae.

Anther Part of a stamen that holds the pollen.

Cell Living things are made up of cells, which are often described as the building blocks of organisms.

Cellulose A tough substance that lines the walls of plant cells, giving them strength and structure.

Creeper A plant that grows around another plant.

Fern Plants with feathery fronds. They do not have flowers, and they produce spores rather than seeds.

Fertilize When a male sex cell joins with a female sex cell. After fertilization, a seed may grow.

Fibonacci series A number series in which each number is the sum of the two numbers before it, e.g. 1, 1, 2, 3, 5, 8 etc.

Floret A small flower that is one of many that make up a flowerhead.

Frond A leaf-like part of a fern.

Germination When a seed begins to grow.

Liverwort A simple plant with leaves that have lobes. Liverworts live in moist places and do not grow flowers.

Mould Fungi that are commonly found growing on food or decaying matter. They are very small organisms, but can grow into large colonies and cause disease.

Nectary Part of a flower that produces a sweet liquid called nectar. Nectar attracts insects to the plant.

Nutrient A substance that helps an organism to live and grow.

Ovary The female part of a plant that makes, and holds, the eggs.

Oxygen The gas that is produced by plants, and that animals breathe to live.

Photosynthesis The process by which plants use the Sun's light to make food.

Pollen The yellow dust on a flower's stamens. Each pollen grain contains a single male sex cell. If it combines with a plant's egg, the egg is fertilized, and a seed can grow.

Pollination When pollen is transferred to the female part of a flower.

Seed A plant's unit of reproduction. It can, in the right circumstances, grow into another plant.

Silica A tough mineral that occurs naturally in some plants.

Spore The unit of reproduction for some simple plants, and fungi. Spores can, under the right circumstances, grow into plants.

Stamen The male part of a flower. It has two parts: a filament that is topped by a pollen-coated anther.

Stigma The female part of a flower that receives the pollen during pollination.

INDEX

NOTES FOR PARENTS AND TEACHERS

Photography and microscopy are two ways in which the physics of light and lenses can be applied to our everyday lives. Use the Internet* to find diagrams that show how lenses bend (refract) light that goes through them. Look at diagrams that show both convex and concave lenses, to discover how the shape of the lens changes the effect. Together, you can work out which of these two types of lens is used in microscopes, telescopes and binoculars. You can also use the Internet to explore the role of lenses in the human eye, and how corrective lenses in spectacles are used to improve eyesight.

On a sunny day, you can demonstrate the focusing power of a lens. Hold a magnifying lens just above a piece of paper that is laid out in sunshine. Angle the lens until the light is focused on the paper, as a small bright dot. As it heats, the paper will smoke and burn.

It is easy to make a water lens that shows how even a simple lens can magnify images. Lay a piece of clingfilm or other transparent plastic over a piece of newspaper text. Use a syringe or a teaspoon to place a single drop of water on the plastic. You will notice that the text beneath the water drop is magnified. Find out what happens when you make the drop bigger, or smaller.

Help children to explore the ways we all use plants. Discuss how wheat seeds and yeast are used to make bread. Find out how cotton grows, and is turned into fabric. Identify how many ordinary items, such as pencils, paper and bedsheets, are made from plant materials.

Examine plants together. Many naturalists discover a love of nature as children, simply by observing plants and the animals that visit them. Sketching and photographing plants help to develop these observation skills.

Teach children to respect the wildlife around them. They can watch wildlife without harming it. Encourage them to respect plants as animals' habitats and food sources, and to disturb the environment as little as possible. Remind them that some plants can sting or are poisonous, so they should exercise care.

*The publishers cannot accept any liability for the content of Internet websites, including third-party websites.